ARTICULATING YOUR UU FAITH

ARTICULATING YOUR UU FAITH

A Five-Session Course

Barbara Wells and Jaco B. ten Hove

Unitarian Universalist Association
Boston

Copyright © 2003 by the Unitarian Universalist Association,
25 Beacon Street, Boston, MA 02108-2100. All rights reserved.

Printed in the United States.

Cover design by Suzanne Morgan

Text design by WordCrafters

ISBN 1-55896-451-7

10 9 8 7 6 5 4 3 2 1

06 05 04 03

Permission is granted to photocopy all handouts in this book for use in this program.

CONTENTS

Introduction	vii
Session One	1
Session Two	5
Session Three	9
Session Four	13
Session Five	17
Alternate Session	21
Handouts	23
What Do I Say After I Say, "I'm a Unitarian Universalist"?	23
Principles as Pillars	29
Articulation Angles	31
Principles of a Free Faith	33
The Choosers Are Chosen	37
A Community for All Souls	45
Coffee Hour Chat Worksheet	51
Short Statements About Unitarian Universalism	53
The Flaming Chalice	55
Resources	57

INTRODUCTION

Discover how news about this course spread through word of mouth. This section offers background on the course, tips for course leaders, and an overview of the session structure.

The idea for this program began in informal conversations with thriving young adult communities at UUA General Assemblies in Rochester, New York (1998), and Salt Lake City, Utah (1999). The participants responded eagerly to some gentle prompts about articulating their faith—not only were they interested in our ideas, they had many of their own, and they were quite willing to share.

Throughout the course of our ministries (now thirty-two years, combined), we have heard persistent complaints about how hard it is to describe Unitarian Universalism. Some variation of the question "What do we tell people when they ask us about our religion?" has probably been directed at many UU leaders many times over many years. This curriculum stems from such questions and our responses to them. Yes, talking about a noncreedal liberal religion like ours can be difficult—but worth the effort! With gratitude to others who have urged us along this path, we have developed some hopefully helpful ways to encourage folks over the hurdles that might keep them from expressing their UU faith to others.

Unitarian Universalists of all kinds can be hungry for ways to articulate their faith. Those who grew up in our movement may not have the inner tools to talk about their heritage. Others coming into the faith (from a different religious background or none at all) could be willing to share their emerging beliefs but might struggle to find appropriate language. Both kinds of UUs can field challenging inquiries from their friends and family about our nondogmatic liberal religion.

We hope this offering will provide Unitarian Universalists the opportunity to explore ways they can better articulate and thus spread the good news of this empowering but demanding faith.

We sincerely thank the many young adults and others who participated in the courses that led to this publication. In particular, we appreciate the good people of the congregation we serve, Paint Branch Unitarian Universalist, in Adelphi, Maryland, who participated in the first field test of this expanded program. We also thank a rich bunch of D.C.-area young adults who helped us in a concentrated field test. We are very grateful to Jesse Jaeger who, during his last year at the UUA Young Adult/Campus Ministry Office, asked us to expand the course and supported us along the way. And, of course, we celebrate the many UUs, particularly our colleagues in ministry, who, throughout our lives, have taught us the meaning of this noble faith by articulating it to us and encouraging us to do the same. This course is dedicated to you.

CREATING THE COURSE

Articulating Your UU Faith is designed to help all UUs speak more effectively about our liberal religion and their particular perspectives on it. It can be used with a mixed group of UUs or with a narrow demographic group (e.g., new members, youth, young adults). While new members certainly find the course helpful, longer-term members also enjoy and benefit from it.

Articulating Your UU Faith works best with a critical mass of people. (It is most effective with ten to twenty participants, but can successfully be adapted for any number between six and thirty.) If the course is well publicized in advance, it will likely attract a good turnout. Each UU group that offers this curriculum will use different tools to publicize it. (Common ones are newsletters, Sunday bulletins, fliers, catalogues, etc.)

It is especially productive for leaders to make personal invitations to potential participants. There is nothing like a well-written letter or a phone call to encourage participation. You might want to use the following blurb to describe the course in publicity materials:

> The focus of this curriculum is on articulation—*practicing* how and what to say in various settings in which you might be called upon to declare yourself religiously or illuminate some angle on this liberal religious movement that has touched and changed so many lives for the better. Such moments are precious opportunities to deepen your own path and perhaps grow a happy awareness in someone else about this rich "living tradition." Yet many of us struggle to describe our religion adequately to others. This course provides hopeful inspiration and resources, plus the opportunity for meaningful connection to fellow UUs.

While settings for the course will vary, it is generally wise to begin publicizing the course about six to eight weeks before it begins. Some places schedule their rooms far in advance, so you may want to reserve proper space before beginning to advertise. The course works best in a room with wall space for brainstorming and adult-sized chairs that can be arranged in a semicircle. The room size may well limit the number of participants.

Some form of registration process can also be advantageous. Once again, groups will differ in their approach to this, but it is often helpful to have some sense in advance of the number of participants. (This is especially relevant for copying handouts and also important if you are planning to provide childcare or a meal.) A small fee for the course can also serve as an incentive to commit and attend (plus cover the cost of handouts, refreshments, and childcare).

Leadership

Good leadership is essential to the success of this course. That said, any experienced and committed Unitarian Universalist with reasonable facilitation skills and a willingness to do some homework can be an effective leader.

Leaders of this curriculum will need to both encourage others and prepare for each session. This work is likely to strengthen their own UU identity and voice.

Leaders should have a good grounding in Unitarian Universalism and be able to articulate the basic principles of our faith. They should also be reasonably knowledgeable about UU history and theology. Those who are relatively unfamiliar with UU history, its contemporary embodiment, or both, could invite a resource person (e.g., minister, seminarian, or knowledgeable layperson) to attend and stand by to help (without dominating, of course).

Articulating Your UU Faith will work well if taught by coleaders (male and female, preferably). This is not a requirement, but coleadership is a good model that allows a less experienced leader to learn along with the participants. A second coleader can also help cover incidental logistics (such as orienting latecomers) and provide backup in case of illness. Plus, a variety of leadership styles encourages a broader range of participants.

The two most important leadership elements in this course are mastery of content and facilitation skill. These could be split neatly between two people. However, good leaders may have abilities in both areas, in which case they can alternate as desired. They should also read ahead through the outline and all the exercises and have a clear picture of how to design the course for their setting.

To provide for deeper content resources, as necessary, the course could include (or perhaps be cotaught by) a minister, intern, director of religious education, or experienced layperson. The opportunity to lead this course would be a very good excuse for someone to pursue an intentional study of Unitarian Universalism.

While the outline gives a sense of the course's flow, a good leader will tailor the course in response to how things are actually unfolding, since each group will differ somewhat in what excites them about the material. The leader will need to know how to brainstorm efficiently, how to honor quieter participants, and how to keep the class moving and on track. Leading *Articulating Your UU Faith* is a fairly demanding task, but you won't regret it! Thank you for your time and dedication to this mission!

STRUCTURE

Articulating Your UU Faith is a five-session course with an alternate or optional additional session. Each session outline includes a standard set of opening and closing activities, one or two exercises, plus worksheets and/or homework reading, which are provided in the Handouts section at the end of the book.

Individual sessions or exercises may also be adapted for use independently of the course, although they do build on one another. We believe participants benefit most from a commitment to the full five sessions.

Time estimates given in the session outlines are made with approximately ten participants in mind. Some times (such as for sharing exercises) could vary considerably depending on the number of participants. Leaders should make adjustments accordingly.

The five sessions are designed to last ninety minutes each, but could be expanded to two hours by adding more opening and closing time (with socializing and refreshments, for example) and/or letting discussions go longer. The five sessions can fit into a variety of schedule configurations, such as the following:

- An evening a week (for five weeks)
- A weekend retreat (one session on Friday evening, three on Saturday, and one on Sunday morning)
- A weeklong event (each morning, say, for five consecutive days of a conference)

The course concludes with a session to plan a worship service. An alternate session and exercise are included for groups that cannot, or choose not to, plan a worship service.

Italicized text in the exercises can be read verbatim, although a leader may often be more effective by knowing the instructions thoroughly enough to speak them without reciting. Nonitalicized text is generally instruction to the leader(s).

Opening and closing elements can be customized as desired to create an effective course experience for most settings. The strongest program, however, will include all of the items. These repeated elements are important to establish group solidarity, safety, and inclusiveness. They can be adapted according to the needs of the setting and course flow.

Setup and Preparation

Arrange seating in a circle, with some extra room around the leader(s). If large numbers and/or small space prevents one circle, create multiple rings with at least one aisle.

Some exercises require individual writing, while some require group brainstorming. Prepare materials for these activities appropriately—and ahead of time. Leaders are most effective and participants feel most comfortable when the setting is clearly ready and someone greets arrivals personally, without having to scurry at the last minute to cover logistical details.

The handouts provided at the end of the book provide substantial background and a deeper orientation to the material generated by the course. Each of the handouts is to be passed out as a homework reading at the end of a given session. This requires a fair amount of photocopying, but the resulting awareness and common reference points for discussion are well worth it.

Leaders should be familiar with the handouts *before* passing them out to participants. All essays are good background for leaders as well. Specific materials and handouts required for each session are listed in the session outline.

Gathering and Starting on Time

It is respectful to start on time, but still important to accommodate late arrivals. One productive way to do both is to begin with a Gathering Activity that honors those who come on time, but is not essential to the flow of the ensuing program.

The first session begins with some informal questions and answers before the formal program begins. Subsequent sessions will offer Gathering Activities to follow up on the assigned reading, with some possible discussion questions provided.

It's also good to have someone else at the door to greet latecomers, explain what they've missed, and give any initial instructions. If there is no need to welcome latecomers, you may want to skip right to the Welcome and Centering Moment if you need to save time.

Welcome and Centering Moment

Welcome participants warmly and thank them for dedicating a portion of their day to this noble endeavor. Cover any "housekeeping" details that need attention and then invite a few deep breaths together. Explain that each session will begin with a centering moment. Offer your own words that speak to the spirit of that particular time and gathering, or share a brief, inspirational reading (or both).

Good affirmations to choose from are #457, 458, 459, 461, 462, 463, 466, 470 in *Singing the Living Tradition*.

Check-In

A guided check-in, as suggested in this course, can be an important way for people to get to know one another. Usually, participants share in sequence without questions or comments from others. A guided check-in can be especially effective because it introduces a particular focus rather than a vague "How are you?" A focused check-in can also set up or otherwise contribute to subsequent content. Of course, leaders can also invite participants to share briefly anything they might need to acknowledge to be more present at that session at that moment in their lives.

Check-Out

A brief check-out near the end of every session gives people a chance to remind themselves what they have learned, and it can give leaders important feedback. If the group is large and participants are still getting to know one another, have people say their names again as they share, especially for the first session or two.

Pause for a few moments in silence and invite folks to jot down (or note mentally) what they will take away from this session. Then go around the circle and invite participants to share responses. Another version is to ask for a personal highlight and/or anything that didn't work well for that person. (Declaring such things right away can help participants release negative energy and allow leaders to follow up, as necessary.)

Closing Moment

Remind participants of expectations for the next session, such as homework and/or materials needed (e.g., notebook or journal and writing implement). Take time to thank the participants for coming. Offer a brief closing, of your own, if possible. Otherwise, good benedictions and closing words to choose from are #679, 680, 683, 684, 685, 687, 688, 692, 698, 700, 704, in *Singing the Living Tradition*.

SESSION ONE

The purpose of this session is to have participants reflect on and share the experience of talking about Unitarian Universalism, particularly out of their own vocabulary and experience.

Materials

- Nametags
- Writing paper and implements as needed
- Newsprint pad and markers

Handouts

- "What Do I Say After I Say, 'I'm a Unitarian Universalist'?" (page 23)

Gathering Activity
5 minutes

Make nametags, orient early arrivals, etc. Appreciate those who came on time and explain that while others are coming in late (greeted at the door by an assistant or coleader), you'll ask some informal questions that will help get things going. Let them know that a more formal opening will be forthcoming in a few minutes. Meanwhile, ask the following:

Who here was raised UU and where?
What other religious backgrounds are represented among us?
Who here has religiously conservative relatives or good friends? What affiliations? (Compare different types, to build commonality among participants.)
What's your favorite religious aspect of this season? (Sample a few.)

Welcome and Centering Moment
5 minutes

Check-In
10 minutes

Mention that in this first session participants will look primarily at their long-standing and evolving faith statements—the "*your* faith" part of the curriculum. Invite participants to share their names, their religious backgrounds, and also one *positive* religious value or principle they remember being important to them *when they were children*.

Curriculum Overview
10 minutes

Take a few minutes to explain the purpose of the curriculum and your expectations. If you are clear from the beginning, you will likely have better participation and involvement. Tell the group generally what will be covered in the course, talk about the importance of attendance, and make sure to mention any possible concluding projects, such as a worship service presentation. Like any good adult course, *Articulating Your UU Faith* should have some basic ground rules about behavior and participation in the class. You may want to invite the class to determine the ground rules. If you prefer just to present them, here are some recommendations:

> Participation: *The course depends on its participants. Regular attendance is very important. Leaders should be informed of any absences.*
>
> Homework: *The course has a modest amount of homework—mostly reading to begin with, then some creative writing. If everyone completes the homework before the sessions, the class will run more smoothly.*
>
> Behavior: *Class members are expected to abide by our UU Principles, guided by mutual respect, understanding of differences, patience, equitable sharing, common courtesy, etc.*

Long-Standing Credo Statements
10 minutes

Before beginning, tell the class that *credo* is Latin for "I believe." Write, "I have always believed _____" on newsprint in large letters. Tell participants to think of the positive religious affirmations they hold that haven't changed from when they were children, or as far back as they care to remember. Ask them to complete the sentence above. Say it out loud a couple of times.

Invite the group to write down as many one-sentence statements using this form as they can in two minutes, without conversation. They can expand on the check-in sharing or explore a new angle. Remind participants to look generally for *positive* religious affirmations.

When the two minutes are up, have the group divide into pairs and take turns sharing statement(s) for a total of two minutes each. Ask participants to say a bit more about why these beliefs came to their attention. Instruct the partners to listen carefully and offer any short, affirming comments that are pertinent to what they hear. Watch the time and call out when the partners should be switching roles. Back in the full group, ask if anyone had any surprises or ah-has, and take a few comments.

Credo Journey Statements
10 minutes

> *Yes, some core beliefs can indeed guide our lives consistently, but most UUs—even those raised UU—also evolve a belief system as they age. What we believe can change. (This is part of what makes our religion so dynamic and*

intriguing!) So now let's explore some ways we've changed our beliefs over the years.

Write the following sentence on newsprint: "I used to believe _____, but now I believe _____." Ask the group to, without conversation, write down a few ways they might fill in this sentence. Take two minutes, and remind the group to look for positive religious belief statements.

Short Break
5 minutes

If appropriate, invite participants to finish and leave the circle quietly for just a few minutes.

Sharing
5 minutes

Back in the full group, invite folks to reflect for a moment on their writing and choose one statement they feel especially strongly about to share if they wish. Have them stand in turn and share that sentence, without further commentary. (Standing focuses attention for the presenter and the listeners.) Offer participants the option of passing for the moment, but return to include everyone who wishes to speak. Remind them that if they get sparked by listening and think of more journey statements, they can keep writing them down.

When the sharing circle is complete, thank them and acknowledge the power of such an exercise and the importance of these statements. Also note gently if there were statements that still ended up in the negative, adding:

We UUs are often inclined to define our beliefs by saying what we don't believe, which is an important marker, but not the best place to live. That's why it's helpful to attend this course and other opportunities like it, to create an increasingly positive vision of what really matters to us and to get better at naming that vision.

Invite participants to honor this writing exercise and continue to develop these important statements. Suggest that they take their affirmations home and share them with close friends—and see what happens!

Challenge
10 minutes

We've heard about a variety of significant beliefs that have changed over the course of your lives. In those transformations, when your theological understanding shifted, you came to a new resting place, a new awareness of your universe. And that movement might not have been the easiest thing for you to do. But you probably felt like you had to do it to be authentic and truthful. Perhaps you had to change what you believed, but it probably was a hard movement, to let go of something you used to believe, yes?

Mention any specific references to the previous sharing that feel appropriate.

So now, if someone were to say to any of you, "Well, as a Unitarian Universalist, with no dogma or creed, you can believe anything you want, right?" what would be your personal response? Anyone?

Sample a few responses. Repeat the challenge as necessary. Encourage them to be personal and specific, speaking for themselves, although repeating phrases used by others will reinforce the message.

Conclusion
5 minutes

When the moment seems right, affirm that, yes, we have no overarching doctrine that we all believe, and then introduce this sentence as a conclusion:

UUs are free to believe what we must. We get our religious authority from our authenticity.

Expand on this idea, using references from the previous sharings. Invite a few further comments and questions to solidify this message.

Introduce Homework
5 minutes

Hand out the essay for reading before the next session, and say something like:

"What Do I Say After I Say, 'I'm a Unitarian Universalist'?" offers perspective on three particular inquiries: about the Bible, about allegedly believing whatever we want, and about what holds UUs together.

Check-Out
8 minutes

Closing Moment
2 minutes

SESSION TWO

The purpose of this session is to begin to look at how we talk about our shared faith—Unitarian Universalism—and to introduce the concept of the Principles as pillars.

Materials

- Newsprint pad and markers (or some other way to brainstorm visually).

Handouts

- "Principles as Pillars" (page 29)
- "Articulation Angles" (page 31)
- "Principles of a Free Faith" (page 33)
- "The Choosers Are Chosen" (page 37)

Gathering Activity
5 minutes

Make sure any newcomers have the handout from last week and remind people of what they were to read ("What Do I Say After I Say, 'I'm a Unitarian Universalist'?"). Invite informal conversation about highlights and insights from reading this essay. If necessary, prompt with questions such as the following:

Did you find the reading helpful in learning to articulate your faith? If so, how?
Can you proudly claim to be a "heretic"?
Is the most important thing about our faith that "we believe and live as if life matters"?
Have you ever seen Unitarian Universalism diminished in public?
How do you understand the word covenant?

Welcome and Centering Moment
3 minutes

Check-In
7 minutes

Mention that in this session participants will look at their experiences talking about Unitarian Universalism. It begins the "*Our faith*" portion of the curriculum. For this check-in, invite participants to share their names (as necessary) and one thing they value highly about being Unitarian Universalist.

Phrases
5 minutes

Most of us have had the experience of hearing other people talk about Unitarian Universalism from well-informed and not-so-informed positions. So let's quickly brainstorm words or phrases that we've heard used to describe Unitarian Universalism or any portion thereof.

Make sure people understand the rules for brainstorming, which generally include the expectation that anything said is okay and that there will be no judgment or crosstalk. But there's a *twist!* While brainstorming as many words or phrases as possible, invite participants to determine if each word or phrase is generally a positive, negative, or neutral term. Highlight the categories by putting them in three columns or underlining in three different colors, whichever is easier.

Some values are in the eye of the beholder, of course, so don't let the exercise get bogged down in definitions or disagreement. When a word or phrase is in doubt or contested, make it neutral and keep moving. The point is to get as many terms up as possible, not have agreement on all their values.

Ask the participants to pair up with someone else in the group. Ask the pairs to each have a mutual conversation about which words or phrases (from the brainstormed list) they like and would use to describe Unitarian Universalism, as well as those that they wouldn't use. Partners should take turns responding personally to specific terms that touch them in some way. Signal to the pairs when they have only a minute left.

Group Sharing
10 minutes

Call the participants back to the larger circle to share any important insights or particularly strong feelings that emerged. Leave time to suggest the following in conclusion:

Language is sometimes controversial, and people often have strong feelings about words and terms partly because language matters! *Some UUs don't ever try to express their religion because they know this truth—that language matters—and they might not feel confident enough in their own expressions to risk articulating their faith.*

But, as Tom Owen-Towle has written, "there are times when we have to help set the record straight about Unitarian Universalism." Plus, there are often people nearby us who just might enjoy finding out what we already know about this delicious religion, even if we feel as though we know only a little bit. So, we can practice and deepen our abilities to describe Unitarian Universalism accurately through opportunities like this course.

Principles as Pillars
5 minutes

Distribute the "Principles as Pillars" handout and walk participants through it, noting especially the relationship of the first and seventh Principles to the others. (They are statements of *what* we affirm about life—"pillars" that hold up the other five Principles, which are more about *how* we agree to be together.) Be ready to refer to the essay "Principles of a Free Faith," which will be distributed as reading homework.

Articulation Angles
5 minutes

Distribute the "Articulation Angles" handout and ask participants to go around the circle, each reading a bulleted item in turn. Each item is a possible starting point for describing Unitarian Universalism. (As needed, and depending on the time left, you could offer or encourage further illumination of any of those "angles" as they are read.) Ask the group to quickly brainstorm other angles that might work. Have them write these down on the handout.

Short Break
5 minutes

Unpleasant Memories
5 minutes

Invite participants into a moment of silence. Ask them to call to mind an encounter in which they struggled to express something about their UU religion—when they wanted to speak well of it, but instead experienced themselves as clumsy, shallow, or otherwise ineffective. Allow participants about twenty seconds of silence. Then invite them to share their frustrating moments with a neighbor, taking two minutes each. Watch the time and call out when the couples should be switching roles.

Naming Issues
10 minutes

Call the group together and ask for short phrases that capture what was at issue in their frustrating experiences—language, confusion, lack of knowledge, etc. Write on newsprint a capsule phrase or two describing each issue raised. Some questions or phrases that their experiences might elicit are as follows:

> How old is UUism?
> Are UUs Christian?
> Flaming Chalice—meaning?
> Freedom = anything goes, right?
> No dogma!—religion or just philosophy?
> Can atheists have a religion?

This portion of the exercise builds commonality among the participants, who see lots of struggles named and thus might feel less inadequate about their own moments of ineffectiveness. The list of issues generated can become a helpful reference as the course unfolds; perhaps all of the identified items can be addressed gradually.

Happier Memories
10 minutes

Staying in the full group, encourage participants to now call to mind any success stories of rising to meet various articulation challenges. Issue a general invitation to the group to take another brief period of silence to call to mind a time or an encounter when they *did* feel relatively effective in expressing something about Unitarian Universalism. After another twenty seconds of silence, ask for brief success stories. Also, note whenever someone's success story addresses one of the struggles listed earlier.

Use your own knowledge and experience plus the resources listed at the back of this book to address any severely unresolved issues. If you are relatively unfamiliar with UU history and/or faith, invite a resource person (e.g., minister, seminarian, or knowledgeable layperson) to help. Expand or contract this exercise to fit your time frame.

Finish by affirming that frustration in describing Unitarian Universalism is very common *and* that we can all get better at it with practice and encouragement. This is a worthy pursuit!

Introduce Homework
2 minutes

Hand out two more essays for reading before the next session:

"Principles of a Free Faith" elaborates on the distinct value of our first and seventh UU principles.

"The Choosers Are Chosen" is a quick romp through UU history.

Mention any other introductory aspects of these readings that deserve to be highlighted, especially in relation to what has happened in this session.

Check-Out
6 minutes

Closing Moment
2 minutes

SESSION THREE

The purpose of this session is to broaden participants' awareness of UU history and provide some very practical experience that will make them increasingly effective when answering questions about their faith.

Materials

- Any of the books from the resources section that are available

Handouts

- "A Community for All Souls" (page 45)
- "Coffee Hour Chat Worksheet" (page 51)
- Resources (page 57)

Gathering Activity
5 minutes

Remind people of what they were to read ("Principles of a Free Faith" and "The Choosers Are Chosen") and have extra copies available as needed. Invite informal conversation about highlights and insights from reading those essays. If necessary, prompt with questions such as the following:

Did you find these readings helpful in learning to articulate your faith? If so, how?
Do you agree that the first and seventh Principles are pillars that hold up the other five? Why or why not?
Does either the first or seventh Principle animate your life in any particular way?
What stands out for you about our UU history?

Welcome and Centering Moment
5 minutes

Check-In
10 minutes

Ask participants to give their names (if necessary) and share one thing they know about UU history.

Brief Historical Inquiry
20 minutes

As UUs we are often asked questions about our history, yet few of us are as knowledgeable about our history as we might like to be. We have a long and noble "living tradition" that is intriguing and inspirational, so let's take a few minutes to delve just a bit into our heritage.

Explain how important it is to refute those who would identify us as "just a '60s religion" or ask, "Isn't that the Moonies?" Invite comments of interest (from the reading) and further questions about UU history. Offer what answers you (or a knowledgeable resource person) can, and refer as necessary to other reference guides.

This is a good time to mention other resources such as the UUA Bookstore catalogue (or your local congregation's book table, if it has one) and the UUA website (www.uua.org). Provide this curriculum's list of further resources to anyone who would like a copy.

Short Break
5 minutes

Role Play
15 minutes

One way to get better at articulating your faith is by practicing, and some of the best practice comes in simulated situations, relatively real interactions, such as the role play we will now experience together.

Arrange two chairs in front (or wherever participants would be most visible and audible to the rest of the group) so that they face each other, maybe tilted out a little toward the rest of the circle. Explain that one role player, A, is to be him- or herself as a UU confronted by the other, B, a strong (but reasonable) questioner from another religion (or no religion). They are having a serious and friendly discussion about why person A is a UU and what that means. Person B is actively inquisitive and maybe a bit incredulous.

Recruit two participants to sit facing each other. Invite them to use the ideas gleaned in the previous session(s) to try to answer the questions spontaneously. Also explain that at any moment another group member will say "Freeze!" at which point the conversation halts and that new person steps forward, points at one of the players, and takes over that role, picking up quickly right at that moment in the conversation. The replaced person returns quietly to the audience.

If other people seem unwilling or unlikely to participate, you can invite engagement by beginning to tap "volunteers" on the shoulder to step into either role. If you have concerns about this, you can also quietly deputize one participant ahead of time to be the first one to enter into the Freeze Tag portion.

Continue as time permits, but be sure to allow time for the group to debrief about the experience.

Debriefing
10 minutes

Facilitate a discussion using these suggested lines of inquiry:

What worked? When did you feel strong and comfortable?
What didn't work? When did you feel weak or awkward?
How did it feel to be in either role?
What will you do differently the next time the subject comes up?

Introduce Homework
10 minutes

Hand out copies of the essay "A Community for All Souls" for participants to read before the next session.

"A Community for All Souls" looks at our heritage and what is asked of us—a good follow-up to the history discussion in today's session.

Also pass out copies of the "Coffee Hour Chat Worksheet" and explain the writing assignment. Tell participants to imagine they are at coffee hour or some other UU function newcomers might attend. They are talking with a newcomer, who asks a couple of quick, general questions about Unitarian Universalism. Those two questions are on the worksheet. Ask participants to write their responses inside the boxes provided and bring the worksheet to the next session. The goal is to be clear and brief yet thorough and encouraging. Tell the group that this creation is the first draft. The next session will include time to develop it further. Tell participants that another way to get better at articulating their faith is to prepare and even memorize the most important points about their religion so they can more easily call up certain key phrases when they need to say something meaningful about Unitarian Universalism at a moment's notice.

Check-Out
8 minutes

Closing Moment
2 minutes

SESSION FOUR

The purpose of this session is to give participants the chance to share and get feedback on their "Coffee Hour Chat" statements. It is also a time to plan what to do with the fifth session (or to do some closure). If you plan to use Session Five to plan a worship service, you may want to preschedule a potential service date so that you can check and confirm the date in Session Five.

Materials

- Newsprint pad and markers (or some other way to visually post information)

Handouts

- "Short Statements About Unitarian Universalism" (page 53)
- "The Flaming Chalice" (page 55)
- Extra copies of "Coffee Hour Chat Worksheet" (page 51)
- Blank 3 × 5–inch index cards, if the next session is the alternate session

Gathering Activity
5 minutes

Remind people of what they were to read ("A Community for All Souls"). Invite informal conversation about highlights and insights from reading that essay. If necessary, prompt with questions such as the following:

> *Did you find this reading helpful in learning to articulate your faith? If so, how?*
>
> *Are UUs more interested in individual accomplishment than community and institutional development?*
>
> *Can significant community really be created in a place where people conceivably can disagree about almost everything?*
>
> *What does the name "All Souls" mean to you now?*
>
> *Do you have "utopian" expectations of (or hopes for) your UU community?*

Welcome and Centering Moment
5 minutes

Check-In
10 minutes

Ask participants to give their names (if necessary) and discuss briefly how they felt about the process of writing their coffee hour chat draft.

Preparation
20 minutes

Remind people about the "Coffee Hour Chat" writing assignment. If everyone has completed a draft, move on to the next part of the session (and expand to fill the additional time). If some have not done so, use this time to have them write a quick draft while others tinker with theirs. (Offer more blank worksheets for those who want to transfer their drafts during this time.)

Prepare and post a newsprint page (or otherwise postable sheet) that lists the following questions. Tell participants they may want to consider these questions as a guide to the effectiveness of their statements.

> *Is it positive and inviting?*
>
> *Is it more personal than abstract?*
>
> *Does it bring in history or theology?*
>
> *Do you want to mention at least one UU Principle?*
>
> *Can you elaborate on it if the chat continues later?*
>
> *Would it inspire the listener to continue associating with Unitarian Universalism?*

Ask participants to share their draft statements with a neighbor, *who will become an ally in its development*. Let each person take five minutes to read his or her draft and receive feedback.

Watch the time and call out when the partners should switch roles.

Quiet Time to Work
5 minutes

Complete the partnered conversations and establish a five-minute quiet period for participants to incorporate any useful feedback into their statements. Offer blank worksheets, if anyone needs them.

Group Sharing
25 minutes

Have participants stand (one at a time) and ask them the two questions from the worksheet as if you were the newcomer, simulating a real conversation. Challenge them to respond without reading their draft. They can hold it and glance down as necessary, but the exercise is more effective if they try to recall the most vital phrases without using the paper (which they won't have in real encounters, anyway).

Allow some short feedback comments from the group along the way. (Asking the same two questions over and over can become a bit tedious, so be creative in your inflection, etc. The precise wording can change a bit, but keep the subject very close to the worksheet questions.)

You may want to carve up the time allowed for this section by the number of participants, so everyone gets a fair share.

Introduce Next Session Theme
10 minutes

At this point in the course, you may choose to proceed with Session Five at your next meeting, or you may opt to use the Alternate Session, which begins on page 21, as a replacement for Session Five or as an additional session before Session Five.

Prepare for Session Five

Distribute "Short Statements of Unitarian Universalism," which offers examples of similar capsule statements about Unitarian Universalism—a few by ministers and two that were created by UU young adults for a field test of this course. Invite participants to read these later.

Also distribute "The Flaming Chalice," which is offered as a brief grounding in the modern history of our dominant UU symbol.

Emphasize that all the good work done by participants is excellent material around which to craft a worship service that would help inspire other UUs to also approach this challenge creatively. This project would also increase the bonds they have among themselves and with others who would attend the service, not to mention further improve their own articulation.

Read ahead to Session Five and give some other reasons why the group might want to consider committing to prepare and present such a service to another UU group, and what would be involved. Discuss and decide whether to do it. (It is not necessary for all course participants to be involved.) If yes, explain that planning the service will be the focus of the next and final session and invite participants to bring ideas on the project. Even those that may not participate can help plan. If a tentative date has been set, confirm it. Keep in mind that the service need not be limited to a congregational Sunday setting.

If the group decides not to pursue this option, or if it's not possible for some reason, but there's still another session to enjoy, proceed to the Alternate Session outline.

Prepare for Alternate Session

Tell participants that the next session will be devoted to deeper discussion and more practice in articulating their faith. Their homework is twofold:

1. *Go over all the curriculum materials that have been passed out and generated, and return with one topic you want to discuss more deeply.*

2. *Imagine a kind of person who might be new at a UU community setting (not necessarily a congregation) and then, on a 3 × 5–inch index card, write out a short profile of that friendly but inquisitive newcomer. Write clearly enough for someone else to read. Include characteristics such as occupation, religious background and concerns, reason for showing up among UUs, typical questions about Unitarian Universalism, etc. Be creative but not too obscure. The goal is to enable another group member to portray this character in an interactive role play.*

These homework instructions are most helpful if written on a large sheet and posted. Distribute 3 × 5–inch index cards. Make sure participants understand the assignment.

Check-Out
8 minutes

Closing Moment
2 minutes

SESSION FIVE

The purpose of this session is to prepare a culminating worship service for another UU group. You may choose to use the Alternate Session, which begins on page 21, to replace this session or as an additional session before this one.

Materials

- Newsprint pad and markers (or some other way to visually collect and organize ideas)
- One or more copies of our UU hymnal, *Singing the Living Tradition*.

Gathering Activity
5 minutes

Remind participants of the handout distributed at the end of the last session ("Short Statements of Unitarian Universalism"). Invite participants into informal conversation about highlights and insights from reading the statements and from further development of their own statements.

Welcome and Centering Moment
5 minutes

Check-In
10 minutes

Invite participants to share a real-life articulation moment they may have had between sessions of this course or describe someone in their life with whom they'd like to have a conversation about this material (and why).

Worship Service Planning
50 minutes

The experience of learning to better articulate the Unitarian Universalist faith can translate well into a creative and inspirational worship service. Offering statements and other insights from this course can be very empowering to both participants and listeners. Participants may find it particularly satisfying to share not only some statements, but also a bit about the process of creating them.

Explore together how the course material (and any emerging ideas) might be presented or adapted to be part of a worship service for any given setting. Encourage brainstorming to help participants spark off each other's ideas.

Be sure to consult a minister (if you have one) in the process of creating this service. Ministers can be great resources, and while they do not need to be a participant in the service, they will very likely value and support the effort that goes into it. A worship associate or trained lay leader may also be invited into the process.

If the course group was small, it may be easy to give every participant time to speak in the service. Otherwise, consider creating a shared reading that features selected pieces of each person's statement (such as a responsive reading).

Obviously, all congregations have their own standard orders of service and local elements to include. Following are possible service elements. Keep in mind that you are free to mix and match these elements or create your own.

Suggested Order of Service Elements

Call to Worship: One of the statements from "Short Statements of Unitarian Universalism" (handout) or one of the Affirmations from *Singing the Living Tradition*

Chalice Lighting: A participant's personal dedication or testimonial or one of the statements from the "Articulation Angles" handout

Opening Words: The leader of the course may talk about the process of creating the service and why it is important to be able to articulate your faith.

Suggested Hymns/Songs (in *Singing the Living Tradition*):

#6	Just as Long as I Have Breath
#118	This Little Light of Mine
#128	For All That Is Our Life
#193	Our Faith Is but a Single Gem
#194	Faith Is a Forest
#287	Faith of the Larger Liberty
#318	We Would Be One
#352	Find a Stillness
#354	We Laugh, We Cry
#360	Here We Have Gathered
#379	Ours Be the Poems
#391	Voice Still and Small

Presentation: Depending on the number of participants, you may choose to have all read their statements as the sermon part of the service. (It helps to put a piece of music between sets of speakers if you have many.) It can also be effective to invite two or three participants to share not only their statements but something about what it means to them to have been a part of this course.

Responsive Reading: You may want to create a multivoice reading based on the statements from your group. (Do not underestimate the power of hearing the congregation read *your* words out loud together.) Be creative!

Closing Words: This could again be done by a leader of the course, summarizing the value of the course (and of Unitarian Universalism), possibly including one of the benedictions and closing words from *Singing the Living Tradition*. However, ensure that some portion of the closing is personal to the course participants.

The service can explicitly encourage other people to expand their own capacities for articulation. If possible and appropriate, announce the next offering of this course. (One of the current participants might consider coleading it!)

If at this point you discover that you need additional meetings to further develop service ideas or address logistical issues, schedule them.

Extended Check-Out
15 minutes

Ask participants to share at least one important thing they learned from this course. Then go around the circle again and invite people to say words of thanks to the group, as appropriate.

Closing Moment
5 minutes

ALTERNATE SESSION

The purpose of this session is to discuss more deeply some relevant topics generated by the participants and to have more articulation practice (and fun). It may be substituted for Session Five, or it may be used as an additional session before Session Five.

Materials

Participants need to bring their homework (chosen discussion topics and 3 × 5–inch index cards of character profiles).

Gathering Activity
5 minutes

Remind people of the handout distributed at the end of the last session ("Short Statements of Unitarian Universalism"). Invite informal conversation about highlights and insights from reading the statements.

Welcome and Centering Moment
5 minutes

Check-In
10 minutes

Invite participants to share a real-life articulation moment they may have had between sessions of this course or describe someone in their life with whom they'd like to have a conversation about this material (and why).

Discussion
15 minutes

Ask the group to turn in their 3 × 5–inch index cards now, but say that you will begin the session by considering a few topics that the group would like to talk about some more.

Ask for a subject, issue, or question that any participant feels strongly about, and facilitate a discussion on it for a few minutes. Then invite another. Play this process by ear, judging when to move on to a new topic. Since there may well be more than you have time for, don't linger too long on any single issue.

Whenever a new topic is brought up ask if anyone else brought a similar idea so that you can combine appropriately and know about how many others are left to consider. Remember that there will be another period of discussion after the role-playing exercise. You may decide to have only one discussion session, if that seems better.

Multiple Role Plays (and a Break)
20 minutes

This exercise will involve a similar motif to the earlier role play (one person plays him- or herself as a UU and another portrays an inquiring newcomer), only this time the group will not focus on one couple interacting. Assign half of the group to each role. The setting is a coffee hour, or some other kind of informal, mingling atmosphere.

Tell the participants playing newcomers to express themselves and their questions as best they can from the perspective of the character profiled on the card they receive. They should be friendly but inquisitive. Participants playing themselves should do their best to respond articulately to the inquiries of the potential UUs. Aim to keep the group in pairs, but if it happens naturally, trios can form as well.

After a few minutes of this, have participants trade roles and hand new cards out to the next round of characters. Ask if there are any questions. About five minutes later, call for attention, collect the cards, and hand out new cards (or some of the same ones, if necessary) to the participants who were themselves in the last round. Turn them loose again.

After another five minutes, announce a short break for those who want it. If you have enough time, extend the interactive periods.

Discussion
15 minutes

Re-form the group and facilitate another round of discussion, which can begin with any processing from the latest role plays and cover more of the specific topics that participants brought to this session.

If you have inserted this session into the course before Session Five, turn to page 17 and introduce the theme for Session Five as instructed there. If this is your final session, proceed as follows.

Extended Check-Out
15 minutes

Ask participants to share at least one important thing they learned from this course. Then go around the circle again and invite people to say words of thanks to the group, as appropriate.

Closing Moment
5 minutes

Handout

What Do I Say After I Say, "I'm a Unitarian Universalist"?

Who are these Unitarian Universalists, standing around the coffee table on Sunday mornings, discussing last night's movie and next Fall's election; reviewing the morning's sermon, designing tomorrow's educations, storming over next century's oceans? [They are] Joyful celebrants of the gift of life, mixing nonsense with the quest of the ages, turning secular need into concerned action, serving wine on the lawn and petitions in the foyer!

—Betty Mills, quoted in *A Chosen Faith*
(edited by John A. Buehrens and Forrest Church)

All my life people have been asking me what it means to be a Unitarian Universalist. Sometimes I have used others' words to describe it, like the ones that came to me on an e-mail recently. This list declared, among other things, that you may be a Unitarian Universalist if

you think socks are too formal for a Summer service.

even your goldfish gets to vote on family TV viewing choices.

you find yourself lighting a chalice before brushing your teeth, etc.

Other times I have used songs or poems. But most of the time I, like you, have had to struggle to come up with my own words to describe this faith I have spent a lifetime committed to—and I can assure you, it hasn't always been easy.

Unitarian Universalism is a different kind of religion, and how we talk about it will thus reflect these differences. Herein I hope to share with you some ideas that have emerged for me over the last decade, ideas that have helped me to better share my religion with others.

Despite the fact that over and over again we hear people tell us, "I sure wish I'd learned about Unitarian Universalism sooner," many of us are reluctant to tell people about our church. Yet churches and church-related communities grow most (and best) when people bring their friends. But talking to our friends about Unitarian Universalism can be daunting.

Let me begin by telling a story. Once upon a time, you, or someone like you, started coming to church or a church-related group. Perhaps you had been away from this kind of thing for a long time. Perhaps you found yourself hungry for some unnamed something that was missing in your life. Perhaps your child began asking questions you couldn't answer without the answer sticking in your throat. Perhaps you went back to the church of your childhood but found that you no longer belonged there.

Searching for a place to belong, you made your way to a Unitarian Universalist church or group. Entering into the place, perhaps you found yourself feeling peculiarly comfortable, energized by the ideas, warmed by the hearts of the people around you, encouraged by the commitment you saw to values not unlike your own. Perhaps you even felt as though you had "come home," so you began attending regularly and getting involved.

Now our story heads toward its critical moment. One day, at your office, or at a dinner party, or at coffee with friends, it slips out that after all these years you are again connected to a church. One of your friends or coworkers asks you, "I don't know much about Unitarian Universalism. What is it you believe?" The fateful question has come. You may stumble, blush, and stammer out a few words about what you don't believe, make a joke or two about it. Then you may give up. Your friends give you a look that makes you feel two feet tall. You go back to the church or group that you find so meaningful, hoping someone like me will help you come up with a better answer for the next time.

Does this story sound familiar? If it doesn't yet, I imagine that you will find yourself in such a position at some time. Unitarian Universalism is a difficult religion to explain if you approach it from the perspective of traditional religions. What I hope to do here is to give you some tools that might make talking about this faith of ours a bit easier.

Before I do, however, I must own up to my own situation. Unlike most of the people in our congregations, I am a born and bred UU. For my entire life, I have found my religious home within this faith. That does not, however, make me immune to the difficulties presented in my earlier story. I too have struggled with language to describe the deeply felt convictions I hold in my heart. I too have been known to tell others first what I don't believe, instead of focusing on the positive aspects of my religion. I too have felt that awkwardness when faced with someone proclaiming firm convictions of the conservative or fundamentalist variety, who cannot understand my faith, filled with ambiguity and diversity as it is.

I imagine that an evolving faith—as ours is and I trust always will be—brings with it the possibility of faltering words, changing viewpoints, open-ended questions and answers. The challenge before us is to creatively find a means to capture our religious values and beliefs in words and symbols that others (and we) can understand.

One way you can begin thinking about this is to consider the concept of *belief*. Most people, including many of us I expect, equate religion with belief. This is not unusual. Many religious traditions are based on belief: belief in a particular kind of deity; belief in a ritual, such as baptism, as a means for salvation; belief in a book or books as the only word of God; belief in a creed that specifies exactly what you must assert as true in order to belong or be saved. Beliefs are important, and all of us have beliefs that we hold dear and that help us live our lives. But belief is not the collective identity of what our UU religion is about.

Many of you may not realize it, but the root of the word *religion* comes from the same root that gives us the word *ligament*. What's a ligament? It's a part of our body that ties our muscles to our bones. So what's a religion? It's that which ties us together. Religion does not equate necessarily with belief. Rather it is something that binds us together.

For some religious people, beliefs *are* what bind them together. But for Unitarian Universalists, what binds us together is not belief but rather our perspective, or our attitude toward life. Whereas others see their religion as based on a particular set of beliefs, our religion begins with a set of affirmations about life, about the universe, about humankind. Our Principles and Purposes Statement states these affirmations quite beautifully, and that is why they are often prominently displayed in our common spaces.

Unitarian Universalism begins with the deep-seated conviction that human life is valuable. We do not set people apart into groups of saved and unsaved, but rather we affirm the dignity and worth of all people. This is our first UU Principle.

With this perspective, we are compelled to treat others with compassion and to work for justice for all people. This worldview may be based for some of us in a belief that the spirit of God loves all people, or in a belief that there is a spark of divinity in all people, or in the simple truth that goodness can dwell in every human heart. From any of these angles, we cannot easily dismiss the "other" as less than human. Thus we are challenged to live with others in peace and as much harmony as we can muster.

Our principles also remind us that the world is interconnected. The earth, the stars, the universe—these are not separate from us; they *are* us. As seekers of truth, we have the wisdom of scientists and philosophers to teach us the deep reality of existence—that we are made of the same stuff as all living creatures, even inanimate life. We are indeed the stuff of stars, and our religion honors this interconnectedness.

This perspective, from which our religion finds its strength, is simple yet also complex. Let me take a few moments to dig a bit deeper and offer you three responses you might give to your friends after you say, "I'm a Unitarian Universalist."

The first question your friend might ask is, "What Bible or religious text do you believe in?" This question has to do with the source of our religious faith. We list six of these sources alongside the Principles because they are enormously helpful in reminding ourselves of the depth and breadth of our religious tradition. These sources include scripture, but they also include our own experience and the experience of others as a guide to truth. One hymn writer over a century ago perhaps said it best when he wrote,

> Lo, that word abideth ever, revelation is not sealed;
> Answering now to our endeavor, truth and right are still revealed.

Truth and right are still revealed. In other words, while what others have written and said over generations is important and may be valid to our current understanding, there is always more to learn. And what we are learning may take the form of revelation in the most spiritual meaning of that term.

Let me give you an example of this kind of revelation. When the first astronauts orbited our planet, they saw Earth in a way that no one had ever seen it before. That picture of Earth floating delicately in space was a revelation to many. It has only been in this generation, however, that that image was available to us. Yet what a difference it has made! Many of us who are committed to protecting our home planet feel this way in part because of the deeply religious image of Earth seen from space. That newer revelation cannot be found in any scripture, yet its effect is profound and, I hope, lasting.

So when, at that mythical dinner party, when your friend asks you about Unitarian Universalism, perhaps you might say this:

> For us, when it comes to religion, the book is open. As an evolving species on an evolving Earth, we are committed, as religious people, to

continue learning, to continue seeking, and to accept new revelation that is bound to come. We find revelation in books, in people, even in photographs, for the holy can touch our spirits in ways we may never have dreamed.

The next question we are asked may sound something like this: "I understand UUs can believe anything they want. Is that true?" This question, believe it or not, has to do with heresy. I love telling people that I am proud to be a heretic, although this statement has been known to take a few by surprise. Heresy, in many people's minds, conjures pictures of those who would not accept orthodoxy and tradition. Well, we certainly fit into that category, historically. Our spiritual ancestors were those who questioned, who challenged, who listened first to the inner voice within calling them to what they saw to be the truth.

The word *heresy* derives from a Greek word that means "able to choose." This is a very important aspect of our faith. If, as I said earlier, we operate out of the assumption that revelation is not sealed, then we have the capacity and the responsibility to choose our religious beliefs as they are revealed to us.

Yes, people say of us that we can believe anything we want to, but this is not true. As Unitarian Universalists, we believe what we *have* to believe—what our senses, our learning, our Earth, our communities, and our wise people teach us we *must* believe. We could *want* to believe the planet is flat, but that would be against what we have learned to be true. So we choose instead to believe what we know to be true: that the planet is round and that we are a part of its life.

So when your companion over coffee asks you that difficult question, another response could be:

> We espouse a religion that honors our responsibility and capability to choose. Because we know that others too must do their own choosing, we value diversity and try to embody a loving acceptance of life's differences. We take responsibility for our religious choices and change them if new knowledge or understanding deem it appropriate. We are heretics, yes, but heretics who believe that the holy is found not in conformity, but in the wide diversity that makes life and our living it so wonderful and rich.

Your friend is not quite satisfied, and asks further: "If your church affirms that revelation can come from many sources, and that you must responsibly choose what you will believe, what holds you together? Do you have a basic belief that undergirds your religious life?" This is a very important question, but one that has, I believe, a simple answer.

Unitarian Universalism is built on a foundation that can be stated like this: We believe and live as if life, indeed all existence, matters. As living creatures, we have been blessed with the greatest gift of all. We did not ask for it, we do not deserve it (any more than anyone else does), yet it is ours to make something with. Life matters not because people alone matter; it matters for itself alone. And because it matters, we find ourselves living life in a way that enables us to make the most of this great gift.

We do this by learning, by choosing, and by giving thanks. We do this by recognizing that our lives, while valuable, are no more or less valuable than the life of any other person. We do this by honoring the life of our Earth, not just human life. We do this by truly living in this world. While we may have varying opinions about the possibility of life beyond death, our faith teaches us that it is in *this* life that we can make a difference.

The price tag for this great gift of life is death. Forrest Church, one of our most prominently thoughtful Unitarian Universalist ministers, reminds us that religion is our response to the dual reality of being born and having to die. Throughout our lives, we will struggle to understand the meaning of both. But if we live as if life matters, we can face death with the certainty that while we lived we did the best we could. And then we can be content with the mystery of what comes next.

The party is over and your friend turns to go. Perhaps you have not converted her to your faith. After all, that was not your intent. She may be happy in her own church. Or maybe she is thinking, "Your faith is not like mine, but wow, have you got faith!" Or maybe, just maybe, she asks to go to church with you and you say, "Wonderful! Let's do it!" Unitarian Universalism is a faith that uplifts and sustains many of us through the fullness of our lives.

It is my hope that you will find acceptance in this liberal religion; that you will feel encouraged to listen to what your heart is teaching you; that you will feel challenged to accept the choices you must make along your journey through life; and that you will feel blessed by the gift of life and live your life alongside others as if they and you, and the whole of creation, matter.

For you do, we do, it does. Let us give thanks for this great gift.

Barbara Wells

Handout

Principles as Pillars

Our first and seventh UU Principles are statements *of what* we affirm about life. They are pillars that hold up the other five Principles, which are more about *how* we agree to be together.

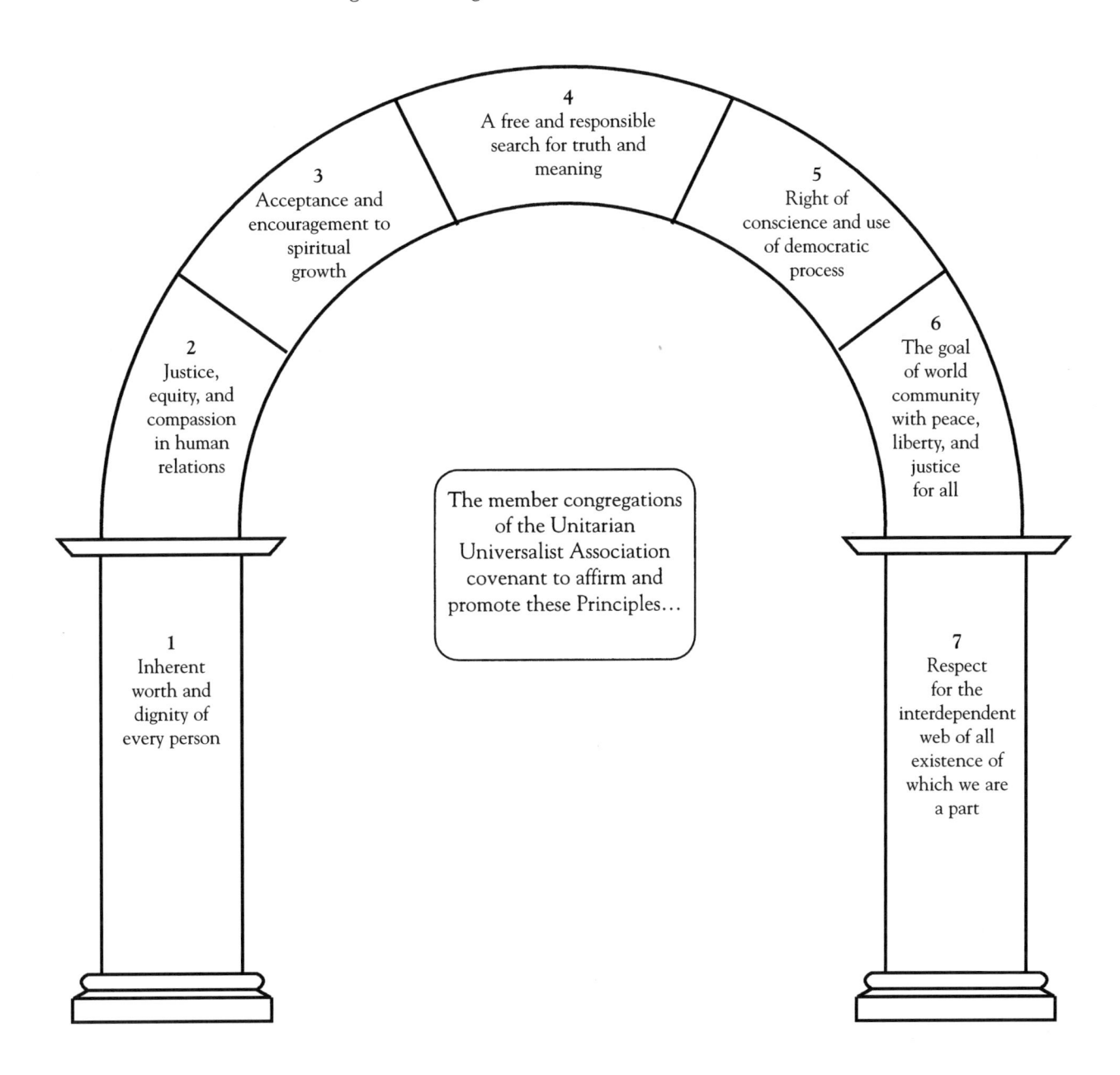

4 A free and responsible search for truth and meaning

3 Acceptance and encouragement to spiritual growth

5 Right of conscience and use of democratic process

2 Justice, equity, and compassion in human relations

6 The goal of world community with peace, liberty, and justice for all

The member congregations of the Unitarian Universalist Association covenant to affirm and promote these Principles…

1 Inherent worth and dignity of every person

7 Respect for the interdependent web of all existence of which we are a part

Articulating Your UU Faith © 2003 by the Unitarian Universalist Association

Handout

Articulation Angles

Consider these helpful angles when articulating your faith:

- UUs are generally united about guiding principles, but very diverse on speculative matters. We try to unite more around behavior than belief. What matters most is not always *what* we believe (content), but *how* we live out whatever it is we believe.

- The word *religion* is from the Latin *religare*, meaning "to bind back or together," as in "ligament." Religion, therefore, emerges in shared values (whatever binds us together), not just shared beliefs.

- The word *worship* is from the Old English *weorth*, meaning "worth," plus *scipe*, meaning "to shape." Worship, therefore, refers to shaping what is of worth, as in friendship, ritual, community, etc.

- If asked, "What do you believe?" first clarify "you." (No one can speak conclusively for Unitarian Universalism as a whole about belief issues.)

- UUs generally honor the mystery of life as a glorious reality. We happily celebrate that there is still more to learn about the inner and outer universe. We strive to be comfortable with ambiguity even as we seek ever greater clarity and awareness.

- We cultivate an open-hearted approach to what is new or strange to us. We are students and learners "from cradle to grave."

- As Samuel Longfellow wrote, "Revelation is not sealed!" The universe is always unfolding anew. We grow from sharing our faith journeys.

- "I am a Unitarian because I believe that by whatever name we call the source of creation, it is ultimately one. I am a Universalist because I believe that at the heart of creation is the universal spirit of love." (Barbara Wells)

- "A 'free *and responsible* search for truth and meaning' (our fourth Principle) means that we are *free* to believe what we *must*. We derive our authority from our authenticity." (Jaco B. ten Hove)

What other angles can you think of?

-
-
-
-
-

Handout

Principles of a Free Faith

In our hymnal *(Singing the Living Tradition)*, as well as in many pamphlets and other UU publications, you will find our Unitarian Universalist "Principles and Purposes" statement. This statement was written not by a bishop, not by any ecclesiastical order, not even by God. It came out of the hearts and minds of the people who made up the Unitarian Universalist Association in the first half of the 1980s, when these "Principles and Purposes" (and "sources") were written and agreed upon. If you didn't take part in writing them yourself, people a lot like you did.

The Principles are not dogma or doctrine, but rather a guide for those of us who choose to join and participate in Unitarian Universalist religious communities. They help us in the ongoing creation of our congregations, as we covenant to try to live up to the spirit of these Principles.

I suggest that two of the seven Principles form the backbone of our faith; they are the pillars that help define and support our spiritual community. I refer to the first and the seventh, which in my view are the closest Unitarian Universalism comes to a true and absolute faith statement.

The first Principle is the one that affirms and reminds us that all people have inherent worth and dignity. It is this Principle that recognizes our common humanity, our common worth, and even our common ability to screw up. In an address to a large group of Unitarian Universalist ministers a few years ago, the great Christian preacher and social activist William Sloane Coffin reminded his listeners that St. Paul was right by noting that "All have sinned and fallen short of the glory of God." "At least we're one in sin," said Coffin, "which is no mean bond, because it precludes the possibility of separation through judgment. That's the meaning of the scriptural injunction 'Judge not, that ye be not judged.'"

In today's world we are called upon to not throw stones at each other, even when doing so might make us feel better and more virtuous. It is easy to blame others for the violence, the poverty, the debilitating anger that often seems to pervade our world. It is harder to look at ourselves and recognize that we are all both a part of the problem and a part of the solution. However, to really be a part of that solution is, as Paul Tillich once said, to " be grasped by the power of love."

Love is really what the first UU Principle is all about. It is a radical love that challenges us to seek not separation, but relationship and connection. As William Sloane Coffin said later in his talk, "Human unity is not something we are called on to create, only to recognize and make manifest."

If we are to be true to our faith, then we must see our first Principle as a powerful reminder of the strength and dignity inherent in the human spirit, even in the spirits of those with armored hearts. For me, the first Principle is a holy reminder, showing me a path through life that begins with relationship and acceptance, not separation and denial. It is deeply spiritual and imminently practical as it offers us tools for how to live. Respect, worth, and dignity are powerful words, powerful challenges about how to live.

Our seventh Principle is, in my view, the other pillar that supports our faith. It reminds us that we are all a part of the interdependent web of existence. This Principle calls us, as my colleague David Bumbaugh has written, "to a reverence for the world . . . this miraculous world of our everyday existence." Can we seek to move through this world with respect and love for our fellow human beings and also learn that the same basic respect and love must be given to the animals, the trees, the hills, the valleys, even the earth and stones on which we stand?

This is a challenging Principle, for it asks us to see the holy very differently from the way most religious traditions see it. The holy, it reminds us, is not only found in sacred scripture, in religious leaders, in a God that is far away. No, the holy is found right here, in every blade of grass, every drop of rain, every creature that walks or crawls or slithers on this planet. Finding holiness in the everydayness of life is extremely difficult and quite simple. It is difficult because it is so commonplace.

The old saying that you can't see the forest for the trees is relevant here. We often can't see the forest, in all its beauty and interdependence, because we're just looking at trees as commodities, as things to be used. Learning to truly see a tree is a deeply spiritual act, just as is learning to truly see a red-winged blackbird, a dying crocus, or a broken rock.

Yet it can be simple to remember the holiness in everyday life, simple because the holy calls to us if we choose to hear. It really is all around us all the time. It is in our backyards, in our workplaces; it is here right now among us; it is in the rainbow shining in the sky. Our seventh Principle is a deeply spiritual guide, reminding us how important it is to seek the holy in all of life.

These two Principles—affirming the worth and dignity of every human being and seeing ourselves as a part of the interdependent web of existence—are strong pillars for our faith. They are also, in their essence, directly linked. Both of them are really about love—a radical love that knows no boundaries.

The first Principle is embedded in the seventh. If we really are all interconnected in the web of existence, then human beings are inherently part of that boundless love. ("I am part and parcel of God," said Emerson.) If more people believed this way, then perhaps more anger and violence could be prevented. Those who kill or act violently usually believe that no one loves them, and their hearts become armored, unable to love or show compassion toward themselves or others.

Our UU Principles challenge us to imagine and affirm a different way: a path of life that sees the hope in every child, the possibilities in every life. The world needs people and religious philosophies that don't separate the saved from the damned. The world needs congregations in which difference is celebrated. The world needs places where children and youth and adults and elders can gather to learn and mentor each other. The world needs you, your congregation, your Unitarian Universalism.

Many years ago, our religious forebears put our UU Principles into action when they stood up against slavery, worked for the rights of women, built more humane institutions, and challenged those who would lead us into war. Today the world requires of us the courage to stand up once again to injustice and tyranny.

When we live the Principle that all people have worth and dignity, we must stand up to those who would deny the human rights of gay, lesbian, bisexual, and transgender people. If we believe in our Principle that all of life is interconnected, we are challenged to confront corporations that are polluting our water. And when we seek to live the radical love that is at the heart of both of these principles, we can develop compassion not only for those killed, but also for those doing the killing. These and other acts like them are not just good things to do. They are deeply spiritual.

I believe the first and seventh Principles of our Unitarian Universalist faith strongly support the other five Principles, together offering us spiritual and practical guidelines for understanding the message of our religion. If we truly live by these Principles, not only will we be better people, but our world will be a better place.

Barbara Wells

Handout

The Choosers Are Chosen

One of the more helpful UU publications of recent years has been the small but power-packed book by Forrester Church and John Buehrens, originally called *Our Chosen Faith* and then reissued as *A Chosen Faith*. The center word in this title puts forth what I think is the pivotal issue for religious liberals of all eras: choice.

Choice implies the *freedom* to choose, which right away differentiates us from many other religions. The freedom we have to authentically choose the belief system that feels right to us is a great gift. For centuries, most people have been severely restricted in this pursuit, if not viciously persecuted for thinking differently. Free religion like ours was all but unavailable not so many years ago. It is still remarkably invisible to many people even today in this avowedly free country.

I imagine that many of you have fielded sneers and disbelief about "our chosen faith" from others who cannot conceive of, enjoy, or accept Religion Without an Enforced Dogma. Well, don't let anyone compromise your spiritual self-esteem! Ours is actually a *huge* faith—a profound faith we have in each other and in our religious willingness to be on a path together without authoritarian theology. I think it takes great faith to be on such an authentically open-ended and demanding journey.

An alternative to affirming our liberal freedom to choose might be to adopt a posture such as that of a woman who was a firm believer in divine predestination. She believed that all earthly events are already ordained by God and we have no choices at all; we are powerless to do other than live out our part in that Holy Plan. One day she fell down a short flight of stairs, suffering only minor bruises. After composing herself, she announced, "Well, thank God that's over with."

Our movement has definite Christian roots, and some significant branches too. The Christians we call our ancestors were not, however, always popular themselves in traditional settings. Early in my studies for the UU ministry, I got quite an earful of affirmation for our so-called heretical ancestors, largely in a fascinating course called Heresies as Alternative Choices. (The word *heresy* in Greek—*hairetikos*—means "able to choose.") When I later took a semester of Early Church History over at a Franciscan Seminary, I heard the Catholic party line, which of course thoroughly dismissed and condemned many of the same folks.

But it remains the case that we religious liberals can trace our theological ancestors right back to the first centuries after Jesus, when many competing interpretations of his and other teachings were available. Origen of Alexandria, for instance, was the most brilliant theologian of the third century who promoted a very popular view of universalism: salvation for all. (This belief eventually provided the name for many of our churches: All Souls. When Forrester Church and

John Buehrens originally wrote *Our Chosen Faith*, they were ministers at the Unitarian Church of All Souls in New York City.)

Modern Christians rarely acknowledge that this *choice* in favor of a belief in universal salvation actually held sway for many in those years near to Jesus. It was a good example of having boundless faith in the goodness of God and humanity.

However, so thorough was the later eradication of this viewpoint by orthodox authorities that we today hardly even know the name of Origen, who was the first prominent universalist, despite being vilified by the Church. More than a millennium would go by before the seeds of this choice would spring forth again.

Meanwhile, a fellow named Arius came to the Council of Nicea in the year 325 to argue that Jesus was *not* of the same essence as God. This council represented a notable turning point; it established the Nicean Creed and laid a foundation for the addition of the Trinity as doctrine. Needless to say, Arius lost his case and was declared an enemy of the now-Christianized Roman Empire. Out of the Council of Nicea came the establishment of the Bible as the only approved scripture. All other ideas were then declared heretical.

For offering a choice that Jesus was not the same as God, Arius and his followers were persecuted as *anti*trinitarians. Again, as with universal salvation, this idea of Jesus' humanity was essentially crushed, to reemerge a thousand plus years later, although even today those who deny the divinity of Jesus are still being condemned as "Arians."

Both of these early heresies are directly related to our name, *Unitarian* (as in, not trinitarian) *Universalism* (as in universal salvation). It is important to me to recognize that Origen and Arius had legitimate belief systems in those first centuries after Jesus. Unfortunately, what we know of their teachings comes mostly from the writings of those who condemned them, because all evidence of their own work was torched. But they lived important lives of free thought. They *chose* their authentic faith in the face of great opposition and danger.

So many uninformed people today consider our religion to be a recent invention or historically shallow, sometimes even confusing us with the Unity or Unification Churches, which *are* both relatively new entries. I am not amused by this common mistake. Our clumsy double name has a long and substantial heritage of offering choices to Christians of conscience. The faith of Origen, Arius, and other early free thinkers was expansive and impressive, and I try to remember and articulate their stories when I'm faced with someone who diminishes my faith.

Continuing a very broad sweep of denominational history, the modern origins of Unitarianism and Universalism are in the Protestant Reformation of sixteenth-century Europe. *Choice* again is the key word that revived this movement and redevelopment of liberal religious thought, even though the persecution of heretics ("those who would choose") was even more violent this time around. That people would stick to their alternative viewpoints in the face of such cruel opposition makes their stories come alive all the more for me.

Michael Servetus was a Spaniard with medical and legal training who came of age as the Reformation was brewing in the first decades of the 1500s. His considerable intellect could not accept the doctrine of the Trinity as biblically based (which is isn't), and he wrote a well-reasoned refutation in 1531 called "On the Errors of the Trinity." Servetus' intention was to find productive common ground for Christians, Muslims, and Jews. But to his eye, the doctrine of the Trinity was very problematic and exclusive. For his effort he was chased around Europe for two decades during the Inquisition and finally burned at the stake by order of John Calvin.

Servetus, whose name has been taken by some of our U.S. churches (for example, Vancouver, Washington), was a noted author and so his violent death got wide attention, but he was not the first of his era to be so treated for the unitarian heresy. A decade earlier, in Poland, Katherine Vogel was forced onto the fiery stake for freely and regularly confessing a belief in the unity of God. She was eighty years old at the time, and her chosen faith was so bounteous as to be dangerous to the powers-that-were.

Meanwhile, an Italian who lived much of his life in Poland gave his name to a strand of the heresy. Faustus Socinus studied the Bible intently and became a calm, well-respected advocate of the unity of God. Socinus became the leader of one of the first groups of unitarian believers—called *Socinians*—during a short period of religious freedom in Poland, the likes of which that country has not known since. The Jesuits eventually gained control of the country and viciously wiped away all traces of Socinianism. Faustus Socinus himself, at age sixty-five, was dragged from his home and killed by orthodox fanatics in 1604.

The largely untold history of these courageous heretics and their compatriots is inspiring and usually suppressed. I honor them as my spiritual ancestors. It is hard to imagine how slowly doctrinal changes were carved into the fiercely resistant religious landscape of these centuries, and how risky were the choices individuals made in the face of authoritarian power. Huge and violent debates were waged over theological distinctions, with lives hanging in the balance. I don't envy the reformers their task, but I'm sure thankful they carried on with it.

The first official movement named Unitarian emerged in Transylvania in 1568, when young King John Sigismund issued a formal decree of religious tolerance. This opened the door for antitrinitarians to use an uppercase "Unitarian" and think more positively. There have been Unitarians in that region ever since; (eighty thousand or so of them today). Since the 1980s, many North American UU congregations are in sister church relationships with Transylvanian Unitarian groups, offering important moral and financial support.

Unitarians and their free thought migrated (often under duress) to Western Europe, thriving in Holland and surviving in England despite continued harassment. Over in the pre-Revolutionary American colonies, such open-minded possibilities emerged as an alternative to strict, pious, unreasoning Protestantism.

Meanwhile, the seed of Universalism, planted by Origen many centuries earlier, sprouted in England but was almost nipped in the bud. Discouraged preacher John Murray barely escaped the British Isles and carried it westward, to eventually found the American Universalist movement. He first landed on the shores of New Jersey, where there is today a UU conference center called Murray Grove.

It is curious to observe how the two separate portions of our modern name developed in the Northeast. While each offered a very clear—and related—alternative to mainstream Protestant religion, there was a most notable class distinction: Unitarians were primarily the elite Bostonians, a learned aristocracy, pioneering cultural and social advances. Universalists, however, by and large, were out in the farmland, relatively uneducated, humble, working with their hands.

The Universalists held on to more traditional Christian theology and liturgy longer than did the Unitarians. Into the early nineteenth century, the new field of biblical criticism began to have a profound effect on theological discourse, offering even more radical choices, which the Boston (and Harvard) Unitarians were actively exploring.

A beloved minister of the Boston Unitarian movement, William Ellery Channing, led the charge toward a more rational religion by declaring that revelation was not sealed, that the insights of theology grow out of each generation's own experience as guided by Reason. He had "too much faith in the boundlessness of divinity to believe it's chiseled in one set of writings for all eternity." This was a very pivotal turn in the evolution of free religious thought.

Channing turned down the chance to be the first president of the newly formed American Unitarian Association in 1825, and the pace of change quickened. Soon he represented the old guard, many of whom still believed in the miracles of the Bible. Along came Ralph Waldo Emerson and his Transcendentalist peers, most of them out of Harvard Divinity School (a noted hotbed of Unitarianism). By their reasoning, the miracles of Jesus were now unacceptable as literal deeds.

Thomas Jefferson spoke very highly of Unitarianism, although he was not an active member. He had a similar disinclination to believe in miracles, and he carved up a Bible to leave out the parts that didn't make sense to him. What he pasted together has been republished by our Beacon Press as *The Jefferson Bible*.

In 1832 Emerson finally gave up his Unitarian parish ministry because he could no longer in good conscience believe in the Lord's Supper communion he was supposed to conduct at his church. Almost a decade later, another prominent Boston minister, Theodore Parker, went so far as to declare that the message of true Christianity transcended its carriers (i.e., Jesus!) and could be intuited by any individual without mediation by church hierarchy.

For this blasphemy, Parker was subjected to the closest thing to an American Unitarian heresy trial. However, he did not choose to relinquish his ministry, as Emerson had done. Instead, he stayed with the church and went on to wage theological battles against slavery and many other social ills of the day. Theodore Parker is a large character in our history; his words were adopted by President Lincoln to more famously promote a vision of "government of the people, for the people and by the people."

Over the course of the nineteenth century, the traditional framework of Christianity began to dissolve for those who believed they were exploring the forefront of religion. For instance, beginning after the Civil War, in the late 1860s, there was briefly an organization among Unitarians called the Free Religious Association, which left behind almost all Christian trappings. (One of its prime movers had the delightful name of Octavius Brooks Frothingham.) Also worth noting at this moment in time was the appearance of Charles Darwin's immensely influential *Origin of Species*. (Darwin had been raised in a Unitarian home.)

The Free Religious Association planted its early humanist seed and then faded. The years on either side of the turn of the twentieth century were slow going for both the Universalist and the Unitarian denominations, as they stayed nominally Christian. The Unitarians, however, concentrated on developing a broader continental, even global base. In 1893 a Unitarian minister organized the very first meeting of representatives from many of the great world faiths. The Parliament of Religions, convened by Jenkin Lloyd Jones in Chicago, carried Unitarianism forth into waters that were not so much *non*-Christian as *more* than Christian. This global organization still exists today, over a century later, as the International Association for Religious Freedom, with triennial congresses of great value.

Meanwhile, the controversial heresies of the earlier nineteenth century had been noticed and, in some cases, even incorporated by adventurous mainline Protestant churches. One could now go to traditional churches and not have to face quite so much hellfire and damnation or trinitarian configurations. At the turn of the century, traditional Protestant churches were including enough similar theological material to draw back members who saw less of an alternative in the now less distinctive Unitarian and Universalist settings. The choices were no longer so clear. The UU heresies had, to some extent, won the day and been adapted into mainstream settings. The specific appeal of Unitarian and Universalist churches was diminishing.

Then came the first swellings of the contemporary humanist movement, launched by the publication of the Humanist Manifesto in 1933. This was a watershed document, signed mostly by Unitarian and a few Universalist ministers. It proposed an enormous faith in human ability, resisting all speculative theologies. From this point on, our religion veered further away from traditional Christianity. (The increasingly rapid pace of social and religious change might be evident in that it took only about fifty years for this humanist seed to resprout after the initial Free Religious Association, whereas it took 1,500 years to cultivate the pioneering work of universalist Origen and unitarian Arius.)

As part of this humanizing effort, in the late 1940s a new series of religious education curricula emerged that were destined to reshape the thinking of future generations. They were largely the work of Sophia Lyon Fahs, who gets my vote for the most influential UU of the twentieth century. (Maybe I'm biased because I was among the first generation of young people who responded to her approach.)

Fahs created curricula (the New Beacon Series) that for the first time placed Christianity in the context of other world religions. The birth story of Jesus was told alongside that of Buddha and Mohammed and Confucius. Bible stories were presented without mention that Christianity was a favored religion over all others. Children were engaged with material that drew on their *own* experiences, according to *their* developmental abilities; they were not just required to learn by rote the "word of God." It was a revolution that helped us, especially those of us from my generation on, to see Christianity as only one of a number of possible choices in which to ground our spiritual authenticity.

The Unitarian and Universalist circles finally came together in a 1961 consolidation, after discovering that they were each choosing more and more of the same path and could benefit from combining efforts. (It is worth noting too that the youth groups of each denomination had pioneered this development by merging seven years earlier.)

Since teaming up in 1961, UUs continue to chart new religious territory. Among denominations, we are far and away the most inclusive of women at all levels. Our welcome of gays, lesbians, bisexuals, and transgender persons has witnessed for the inherent worth and dignity of all people. We have avowedly pagan groups exploring Earth-centered spirituality. Many of us are actively promoting a religious right to choose various medical options. Antiracism continues to stir us as a challenging goal. UU Christians are still pushing the boundaries of the theistic option. Our time has no shortage of issues that call out for courageous thought, articulate expression, and concerted action.

I'm among those who have been especially intrigued and challenged by the concept of interdependence that we now include in our religious principles. What does it really mean for me to be interdependent with you, with those who speak a different language, with the rain forests, with the whales? How does that realization affect my behavior? These are now religious questions of the highest order because the dual reality of living and dying exists for all the life with which I am interconnected. These are questions that require a fierce and thorough examination of modern diversity. Since I know the value of being able to choose, I must honor that ability in others too.

Today some of us contemporary UUs have chosen to stay in the movement that raised us, others have chosen to return after a sojourn away, and many others have chosen to enter with fresh voices and stories, bringing the vitality that diversity always produces. We are all at once lucky and cursed: lucky for the liberating freedom of conscience possible in nondogmatic religion, and cursed by the unending possibilities that demand our steady attention. It is no easy task to be unfettered by doctrine; we *have* to choose for ourselves. Our religion offers strong principles and tools for that task, but ultimately it is our own activity that makes the difference; it is our own choices that set the stage for our growth.

In a dynamic religious community, we sort things out together as life colleagues, sharing insights and struggles, learning from each other in relationship. This occurs in magnificently different ways in each UU group, yet it always seems to be happening. It has been said that our UU congregations are as unique as fingerprints, and as similar. I agree with Forrest Church when he reminds us that earlier Unitarians and Universalists placed a high value on individualism and freedom because they were fighting to lift the chains of oppression, theological and otherwise. Today we can choose from so many freedoms that the liberation we seek is not necessarily from bondage, but from *bondlessness*. Has the pendulum swung so far that we are now uprooted and alienated from each other amid our extreme freedoms?

Indeed, the frontiers of religion may now involve the harnessing of those hard-earned freedoms into more productive community-building, whatever that is going to look like in the first years of the twenty-first century. The truest, most egalitarian community on Earth is the community *of* Earth. I believe that honest religion of our time will be reflective of this fact.

I wish I could say just what this means, but we are still in the early throes of this latest surge of religious growth. It is an exciting, important time. People deep into the decades ahead will look back on the turn of *this* century and say . . . well, what *will* they say?

I hope Unitarian Universalist ministers giving sermons many years from now describing the latest sweep of their movement's history, will note the following:

- That an awareness of our fundamental interdependence took hold in this era
- That UU communities offered spiritual guidance for their members and maybe even the culture at large as we all lurched into a more responsible relationship with the rest of the planet
- That among this generation there was an animated spirit that ushered in a healthy and creative future

We come to this moment from a long line of innovators, free thinkers, and courageous pioneers who were simply doing the best they could in the spirit of religious pluralism. I'm proud of this lineage and humbled by the tasks before us. But, like William Ellery Channing, I have "too much faith in the boundlessness of divinity" to shrink from simply doing the best I can. That is the heritage of our chosen faith.

Jaco B. ten Hove

Handout

A Community for All Souls

I grew up in the Washington, D.C., metro area, and as a child I always heard a lot about our mother church, All Souls Unitarian, in the District. I remember finding the name very appealing even as a youngster and wondered why more of our congregations were not called by that felicitous name.

Many years later, when I was the minister of a new congregation in the Seattle area, I preached a sermon as we were settling on our permanent name about why I thought that church should take on the mantle of "All Souls Church." I felt that name said so much about what we stand for and who we are. They chose not to follow my advice, but I still think the name "All Souls" is a good one.

Over the years I have continued to reflect on what it would mean for a church to really be a church for all souls:

> to be a church where the door was open wide enough to include people of many different beliefs and backgrounds;
>
> to be a church where being in community meant more than just getting along, where it meant deepening our relationship with each other to a profound level, where real transformation takes place.

Are Unitarian Universalist churches in a unique position to fully live out this ideal? I keep asking myself that question.

Unitarian Universalist ministers generally like talking about our history. This is often because so many marvelous figures from the past are a part of our religious heritage. Many individuals made important contributions to American (and other) history, and we are proud to claim them, yet how many can you name?

Let me ask an even harder question. Can you name any of the congregations, groups, or communities that were historically notable and Unitarian or Universalist? For most of us, when we think about history—particularly UU history—we remember the famous individuals who preached or talked or lived the doctrines of liberal religion. Few of us know of the communities that over time have made a difference in the lives of these same individuals.

There are, of course, reasons for this. History is always more stimulating when we tell the tales of individuals living out their lives in exciting and intriguing ways. Few groups or communities are as interesting as the individuals within them. Yet most, if not all, of the individuals that we cherish so much in our history were nurtured and sustained by the groups and institutions that were their communities.

If you walk down the main streets of many of the most prominent New England towns today, you discover church after church called First Parish, Unitarian Universalist. These congregations—ranging from large churches like the one in Concord, Massachusetts, to small village churches like the one in Petersham, Massachusetts—have served the needs of Americans, some quite famous, for over two hundred years. Yet we usually hear little about them and the role they played in shaping the individuals we hold up as great models to our children.

Take, for example, one of the most famous writers and thinkers of the nineteenth century, Ralph Waldo Emerson, who grew up in a church community as the son of a Unitarian minister. As a young minister himself, he served a church in Boston for a few years, though it is said he did not find the politics of church life much to his liking. But after he quit the formal ministry to establish a career as a writer and lecturer, he continued to preach in a small church in East Lexington (Massachusetts) for many years. In later life he also attended services at the church in Concord. These congregations, seldom if ever mentioned in Emerson's writings, were nonetheless instrumental in his religious and cultural awakening.

Yes, Emerson found the politics of church life difficult to bear. He also believed that the individual is paramount and that God should and could be approached directly, not through the auspices of a minister or the church. This Transcendentalist perspective—that an individual can have a direct relationship to the holy—has become an essential element in Unitarian Universalist theology. We love to quote Emerson, holding up his doctrine of self-reliance as one of the most important concepts of Unitarian Universalism.

But I think we may have missed something here. Despite Emerson's vaunted individualism, his life was lived deep in the middle of community. The town of Concord, his group of friends, even the church that he sometimes scorned were important communities of people to whom he remained attached and committed throughout his life. He may have thought he didn't need community, but he nonetheless lived his life in the midst of it.

Emerson died over one hundred years ago. Yet each of the congregations he touched is still going strong. That's one of the most important things about religious communities. Every one of us will die, but our values and principles can continue on if we sustain them through the institutions we create and support.

None of the churches in Emerson's life were called "All Souls," but throughout their histories they sought to be inclusive communities, or at least as inclusive as they could be, given their era. They are also all historically Unitarian congregations. But our Universalist forebears also tried to create communities that lived out their belief in God's love for all people. Universalism, as it has evolved over the past three centuries, is a doctrine that says that true community is made up of people who come from many different walks of life, all with something to offer. Historically, the Universalists were among the first to try to create communities in which all people were welcome.

One such community was the radical experiment called Hopedale, outside Boston. In the mid-1800s, America was a place where the ideals of freedom and liberty were often talked about more than lived. For instance, women could not vote, people in the South still owned slaves, and the resident population generally despised the waves of immigrants coming from Ireland and other parts of Europe.

Into this milieu came the radical Universalist, Adin Ballou. Ballou became a Universalist in 1823, and he was, in his day, an important social critic. Ballou was convinced that Universalism was a doctrine that needed to be lived as well as believed, and so he imagined a place in which Universalist ideals would be put into practice. His dream was also inspiring to others, and in 1841 the community of Hopedale was formed.

Hopedale was not a church, but a religious community where people lived together following the principles of what Ballou called "practical Christianity." Ballou's vision for Hopedale was that

> the community would not only afford a haven and a refuge from a corrupt church and an oppressive world, but would be a basis for missionary activity. If such communities could be multiplied indefinitely, the reign of ignorance, selfishness, pride and violence would be terminated . . . and the whole great Brotherhood [sic] of our race dwell together in unspeakable peace.

When the community was founded in 1841, Ballou's Universalist idealism led him to insist that its members make very deep commitments to Hopedale. They could not drink alcohol or gamble, had to commit to nonviolence, and were to refuse to participate in the government except to pay taxes. Hopedale grew and, over the course of its fifteen-year life span, reached a peak of three hundred residents.

But it did not last. When two brothers who owned the largest portion of Hopedale shares pulled out, the community collapsed and ultimately became a part of the town of Hopedale, which still exists today. (There is also a Unitarian Parish Church in the town, organized in 1868.)

Perhaps such utopian settings are unrealistic in any generation, but the vision that Ballou held in his heart reached far beyond that small group of people in Massachusetts. Ballou really believed that religious community could be a place where all souls are welcome. At Hopedale, women, African Americans, and others on the margins of society were—at least in theory—welcome to participate at an equal level. (For instance, Ballou said that while women could hold leadership positions, they probably wouldn't want to!) Hopedale attempted to model an environment in which the ideals of Universalism were acted upon—a worthy goal, even if it did not last forever.

Does the Hopedale experiment have any bearing on our UU communities today? Most of our groups are not residential communities of people who come together to live and work in the same place sharing goods and livelihood. Thus, in many ways, we are very different from our Hopedale ancestors.

But I think it's important for us to remember that what happened at Hopedale was valuable if for no other reason than that it showed the world that people could live together in a radically inclusive fashion, even if only for a few years. Our congregations and other UU-related groups generally still uphold that ideal and seek to be places where people of all ages, races, gender, and beliefs can be together in a community of all souls.

A UU church member once suggested to me that one of the most important things he found when he first came to his church ten years earlier was a place where he could be himself with others. He explained how at his work there was a very strict hierarchy, but at church he felt such relief to be in a place where people came together without worrying about where they stood in a pecking order. While he might not have identified it as such, he saw the doctrine of Universalism being lived out, and it made him want to return and become a part of the congregation.

But there are also great challenges inherent in trying to create community in a church with a diverse and inclusive approach to religion. Is significant unity possible where people conceivably can disagree about almost everything? (Don't you imagine that disagreements also happened at Hopedale?)

How many of my own individual beliefs or attitudes may I need to release in order to be in a deeper relationship with people who are very different from me? This gets to the heart of what I see as the challenge embedded in our history. For many of us, what makes being a Unitarian Universalist so appealing is our religious tradition's emphasis on the value of the individual. For most UUs, particularly if we were raised in a more traditional religion, to be given the freedom to think for ourselves religiously is powerful medicine. The ideals of liberal religion also influenced in profound ways the American culture.

But those early liberal thinkers and leaders—such as Thomas Jefferson, Ralph Waldo Emerson, and Adin Ballou—lived in a time very different from our own. They lived in a land with far fewer people than we do today. They lived in a nation where the nearby frontier with all its freedom beckoned constantly. And they lived in a religious world in which the hidebound traditions of the past still held sway even as they were being threatened.

For people like Jefferson and Emerson to hold up individualism as paramount was so liberating that it led to many of the freedoms we now enjoy. It was a very important piece of human progress at that time. But it did not come without a cost. I do not think that Jefferson or Emerson would ever have thought that their beliefs would lead to the kind of rampant individualism bordering on selfishness and isolation that many of us experience today. Certainly Adin Ballou would be appalled. Community, for them, was built into their very lives.

For us now community is not a given. Often our lives are lived in neighborhoods where we know few people in a deep way, in workplaces where the environment may keep us from strengthening relationships, and in families where we might live thousands of miles apart from those we love. For Jefferson and Emerson and others then, traditional communities were assumed. For us they are something we have to work for and create together.

So how do we do that? How do we build community when our religious tradition encourages us to be individuals? Clearly, many people today come to church and church-related groups for "community." We hear that repeatedly from people arriving at services and events. While our liberal theology is certainly an essential piece of why people come here, for many people the community is equally if not more important.

But the kind of people who find Unitarian Universalism appealing are generally people with a strong sense of their rights and responsibilities as individuals. In other words, people come to Unitarian Universalist congregations and groups with strong opinions. When those strong opinions clash, our hope for community may be challenged. We could, like Thomas Jefferson, decide to be "unitarian alone." It isn't hard to be alone these days. We could just as easily sit in front of our computer reading up on all the great Unitarian and Universalist thinkers without ever coming into contact with someone who might challenge or change us.

But for many of us, the pull to be in community is greater than the desire to be alone. And so we come together, giving up a little bit of our individualism in order to be in a deeper relationship with others. It isn't always easy. It never has been, as the Hopedale story reminds us. But no one said the creation of community would be or should be easy! For while a congregation or group may not ask as much of you as Adin Ballou did of his Hopedale members, we can still ask of each other some important things.

In a Community of All Souls, we might ask of each other the following four aspects (among others):

The first aspect is *acceptance*. If a church or group is to be open to all people, we must learn to accept each other in our wholeness. This is the element of individuality that none of us would ever want to lose. Every person is a unique spirit. For us to truly accept one another is to see that uniqueness as a gift even when at times it may drive us crazy. But in our acceptance, we also have the opportunity to expand our horizons about what is acceptable. A church of all souls will be by definition open to new ways of looking at and accepting each other.

The second aspect we must ask of each other is related to the first: *authenticity*. In a true community we have the opportunity to be authentic and real. Our religious forebears fought long and hard to be able to speak the truth as they understood it. In their time, most religious groups told only one truth. But today I suggest that an authentic religious community is one in which we acknowledge one another's differences honestly and lovingly.

In such a place we encourage and support one another as we struggle and work to become more fully who we are. I like to think this is one reason that people in the gay, lesbian, bisexual, and transgender communities generally feel comfortable among us. A church that accepts people in their authenticity is bound to be a place where many people feel welcome.

The third aspect is even more challenging than acceptance and authenticity: *ambiguity*. No liberal religious community is ever going to have all the answers. If we did, there wouldn't be any need for questions, and questions are how we learn and grow. In our various UU configurations, I hope we can be places that accept the ambiguity inherent in life. I hope we can be open to wrestling with the questions life brings. And I hope that we will want to do that wrestling together, for we can learn more by sharing our questions than by just insisting that our answers are correct.

Finally, I hope that we can be a community that has high *aspirations*. We may not want to be a community like Hopedale. Yet what I like about the story of that historical endeavor is that its founders had a dream of being more than they already were. They aspired to be a truly loving and peaceful model for the world. They chose to do it in a way that was perhaps unrealistic and utopian. But just because creating a perfect community may be beyond our grasp doesn't mean we should give up our aspirations to be more than we already are.

Can your congregation or group aspire to be a religious community where all souls searching for authenticity and acceptance are welcomed to walk their path, even amid the struggle with life's ambiguities?

I believe in this vision, but it won't happen without some hard work. It is mighty hard to learn to let go of our prejudices and expectations as we learn to live together in the shared life we call modern community. Yet many good folk seem willing, even eager to make it work. Maybe we recognize that community is worth the price we pay for it. Okay, we can't always have it our way (despite what the advertising jingles would have us believe), but would we rather sit alone in our rightness or be together in a loving (and at times challenging) compromise we call community?

Emerson scoffed at the church and convinced generations of his followers that religion is best experienced alone. Today we've seen the limitations of this approach to the spirit even as we celebrate the ability we have been given to walk our unique spiritual paths. Perhaps what we are finally learning is the balance that enables us to walk together, sharing the journey while carrying our own packs. I like to think that UU settings can be places where all of us backpackers on the journey through life share the path together. That's what I want to be a part of—a community of all souls. I hope you'll join me on the journey.

Barbara Wells

Handout

Coffee Hour Chat Worksheet

Imagine you are at coffee hour—or some other UU function that includes people who are relatively new to our religion. You are talking with a newcomer, who asks you to respond quickly to two general questions about Unitarian Universalism in the course of, say, five minutes. Write your responses in the spaces following the questions. Your goal is to be clear and brief yet thorough and encouraging.

Question 1: So what is this Unitarian Universalism?

Question 2: Okay, you're a UU. What do you believe?

Handout

Short Statements About Unitarian Universalism

Ours is a religion whose theology is unitarian, whose faith is universalist, whose worship is creedless, whose polity is congregational. —Fred Muir, UU parish minister

We Unitarian Universalists have inherited a magnificent theological legacy. In a sweeping answer to creeds that divide the human family, Unitarianism proclaims that we spring from a common source; Universalism, that we share a common destiny. That we are brothers and sisters by nature, our Unitarian and especially our Universalist forebears affirmed as a matter of faith: Unitarianism by positing a single God, Universalism by offering the promise of a shared salvation. —Forrest Church, UU parish minister, from an essay in *The World*, Nov./Dec. 2001

Unitarian Universalists believe in the integrity of universal wholeness, the value of diversity of the unitary parts and affirming the inherent connections each to the other within all existence. —Lisa Wiggins, UU community minister

Unitarian Universalism is a free-thinking liberal religion that is guided by shared values rather than a particular dogma or creed. This gives the individual the opportunity to determine personal beliefs based upon conscience and experience. At its core, Unitarian Universalism places an emphasis on the worth and value of every person and the interconnectedness of all things. UUs are encouraged to give life to their values, demonstrating compassion, respect, and justice, working together to make the world a better place to pass along to our children. —Erika Alston, Arlington, VA

As a cultural phenomenon, I see the Unitarian Universalist movement as a safe and loving sandbox where each individual's spiritual search is encouraged within an interdependent web. Collectively, this is a growing sandbox, both in size as we take actions with regard to our beliefs, and in depth as each person's spirituality evolves together. The free searching that goes on in this sandbox can be seen as a model of the whole source of creation. Considering this sandbox as a part of that whole reveals an exciting self-similarity. This is just one clue to me of many that we're on to something big with this faith. —Darrell Duane, UU Young Adult Organizer, Washington, DC

Unitarian Universalists share many scriptures, not just one, and a belief in the here and now, not just the hereafter. We value freedom, reason, tolerance, and love as overarching values. We honor deeds, not creeds, as we try to live our faith. We believe everyone should be forthright about religious living by using that old ethic from high school math class, "show your work." Ours is an evolutionary theology, understanding that language changes with time and growing awareness. In the final analysis, we believe we are saved by love and made holy by character. —Daniel O'Connell, UU parish minister

Handout

The Flaming Chalice

At the opening of Unitarian Universalist worship services, many congregations light a flame inside a chalice. This flaming chalice has become a well-known symbol of our denomination. It unites members in worship and symbolizes the spirit of our work. The flaming chalice combines two archetypes—a drinking vessel and a flame—and as a religious symbol has different meanings to different beholders.

Chalices, cups, and flagons can be found worldwide on ancient manuscripts and altars. The chalice used by Jesus at his last Passover seder became the Holy Grail sought by the knights of Wales and England. Jan Hus, Czech priest and forerunner of the Reformation, was burned at the stake for proposing, among other things, that the communion chalice be shared with the laity.

More recently, feminist writer Riane Eisler has used the chalice as a symbol of the "partnership way" of being in community. Sharing, generosity, sustenance, and love are some meanings symbolized by a chalice. A flame can symbolize witness, sacrifice, testing, courage, and illumination.

The chalice and the flame were brought together as a Unitarian symbol by an Austrian artist, Hans Deutsch, in 1941. Living in Paris in the 1930s, Deutsch drew critical cartoons of Hitler. When the Nazis invaded Paris in 1940, he abandoned all he had and fled to France, then to Spain, and finally, with an altered passport, into Portugal. There, he met the Reverend Charles Joy, executive director of the Unitarian Service Committee (USC). The Service Committee was new, founded in Boston to assist Eastern Europeans, among them Unitarians as well as Jews, who needed to escape Nazi persecution. From his Lisbon headquarters, Joy oversaw a secret network of couriers and agents. Deutsch was most impressed and soon was working for the USC.

The USC was an unknown organization in 1941. This was a special handicap in the cloak-and-dagger world, where establishing trust quickly across barriers of language, nationality, and faith could mean life instead of death. Joy asked Deutsch to create a symbol for their papers "to make them look official, to give dignity and importance to them, and at the same time to symbolize the spirit of our work."

Thus, Hans Deutsch made his lasting contribution to the USC and, as it turned out, to Unitarian Universalism. It was, Joy wrote his board in Boston,

> a chalice with a flame, the kind of chalice which the Greeks and Romans put on their altars. The holy oil burning in it is a symbol of helpfulness and sacrifice. This was in the mind of the artist. The fact, however, that it remotely suggests a cross was not in his mind, but to me this also has its merit. We do not limit our work to Christians.

The flaming chalice design was made into a seal for papers and a badge for agents moving refugees to freedom. In time it became a symbol of Unitarian Universalism all around the world.

Today the flaming chalice is the official symbol of the UU Service Committee and the Unitarian Universalist Association. Officially or unofficially, it functions as a logo for hundreds of congregations. Perhaps most importantly, it has become a focal point for worship. No one meaning or interpretation is official. The flaming chalice, like our faith, stands open to receive new truths that pass the tests of reason, justice, and compassion.

The story of Hans Deutsch reminds us that the symbol of a flaming chalice stood in the beginning for a life of service. When Deutsch designed the flaming chalice, he had never seen a Unitarian or Universalist church or heard a sermon. What he had seen was faith in action—people who were willing to risk all for others in a time of urgent need.

Daniel D. Hotchkiss

RESOURCES

Many of these books are available in the UUA Bookstore. You can order by calling 1-800-215-9076 or visiting the website at www.uua.org/bookstore. Your congregation's library may have some as well.

UU HISTORY

These works offer an introductory path into our liberal religious heritage:

American Universalism
by George Huntston Williams, fourth edition (Skinner House Books, 2002)
A classic, digestible study of two hundred years of Universalist history in the United States.

A Faith People Make: Illustrated Unitarian Universalist Lives
by Stephen Kendrick (Universalist Church of West Hartford, CT, 1997)
Good capsule portrayals of twenty-one notables, from Priestley to Reeb.

Follow the Gleam: A History of the Liberal Religious Youth Movements
by Wayne Arnason (Skinner, 1980)
A thorough treatment of how Unitarian and Universalist youth organizations evolved and merged into Liberal Religious Youth; with photos!

The Gospel of Universalism: Hope, Courage, and the Love of God
by Tom Owen-Towle (Skinner House Books, 1993)
A thin, but resonant volume of twenty vignettes that reflect on the power of Universalism's guiding principles. This book is out of print.

A Stream of Light: A Short History of American Unitarianism
Conrad Wright, ed., second edition (Skinner House Books, 1989)
A scholarly set of five essays that present five early generations of Unitarianism.

Three Prophets of Religious Liberalism
Conrad Wright, ed., second edition (Skinner House Books, 1996)
A powerful portrayal of the most influential sermons by Unitarians William Ellery Channing, Ralph Waldo Emerson, and Theodore Parker, with good contextual and explanatory material about each.

The Unitarians and the Universalists
by David Robinson (Greenwood Press, 1985)
A concise but thorough summary of our American UU story, with a helpful biographical dictionary.

GENERAL UNITARIAN UNIVERSALISM

These items offer a broad perspective on our faith from a variety of angles:

Being Liberal in an Illiberal Age: Why I Am a Unitarian Universalist
by Jack Mendelsohn (Skinner House Books, 1995)
A venerable set of eloquent and idealistic essays.

A Chosen Faith
by John A. Buehrens and Forrest Church (Beacon Press, 1998)
A very readable introduction to Unitarian Universalism, focusing on the Sources of our living tradition.

Everyday Spiritual Practice: Simple Pathways for Enriching Your Life
Scott Alexander, ed. (Skinner, 1999)
A helpful series of thirty-eight short essays that do what the title suggests.

God and Other Famous Liberals: Recapturing Bible, Flag, and Family from the Far Right
by Forrest Church (Simon & Schuster, 1992)
A stirring set of eight essays that connect liberal religion with democracy. This book is out of print.

Heretics' Faith: Vocabulary for Religious Liberals
by Fredric John Muir available from UU Church of Annapolis, MD, 2001)
An alphabetical collection of concise and insightful essays on fifty-one important religious subjects, including some provocative classic and contemporary concepts.

Our Seven Principles in Story and Verse: A Collection for Children and Adults
by Kenneth W. Collier (Skinner, 1997)
An encouraging, very readable sashay through the seven Principles.

Today's Children and Yesterday's Heritage
by Sophia Fahs (Beacon, 1952)
An inspirational and timeless explication of what serves UU children well. This book is out of print.

The Unitarian Universalist Pocket Guide
John Buehrens, ed., third edition (Skinner House Books, 1999)
The third edition of this popular handbook provides a good overview through eight essays and a chronology of important dates.

What Unitarian Universalists Believe: Living Principles for a Living Faith
by eleven authors (UUA Denominational Grants Panel, 1987; published by All Souls Church, New York, NY)
Excellent early "Resources for Study and Worship," based on the seven Principles.